DON'T LET ANXIETY STOP YOU

Eliminate Anxiety And Panic Attacks With One Simple Strategy, One Step A Day

DISCLAIMER

This document is geared towards providing exact and reliable information in regards to the topic and issue covered. The publication is sold with the idea that the publisher is not required to render accounting, officially permitted, or otherwise, qualified services. If advice is necessary, legal or professional, a practiced individual in the profession should be ordered.

This is in terms of a Declaration of Principles which was accepted and approved equally by a Committee of the American Bar Association and a Committee of Publishers and Associations.

The information provided herein is stated to be truthful and consistent, in that any liability, in terms of inattention or otherwise, by any usage or abuse of any policies, processes, or directions contained within is the solitary and utter responsibility of the recipient reader. Under no circumstances will any legal responsibility or blame be held against the publisher for any reparation, damages, or monetary loss due to the information herein, either directly or indirectly.

Respective authors own all copyrights not held by the publisher.

The information herein is offered for informational purposes solely, and is universal as so. The presentation of the information is without contract or any type of guarantee assurance.

The trademarks that are used are without any consent, and the publication of the trademark is without permission or backing by the trademark owner. All trademarks and brands within this book are for clarifying purposes only and are owned by the owners themselves, not affiliated with this document.

Table of Contents

Clutter

Table of Contents

INTRODUCTION

I want to congratulate you for taking your first step towards freedom from anxiety and panic attacks. Few people take action on their problems.

Anxiety can take several forms. It is an emotion, just like anger, sadness and happiness, and is felt by all of us at some point in our lives. Symptoms for mild anxiety can be bodily sensations like butterflies in the stomach, sweaty palms and forehead. Everyone has experienced at least one of them at some point in their lives. It is normal to feel anxious from time to time. However in some cases anxiety takes a notch up in level with symptoms to match, this uncommon form of anxiety in people is then termed as an anxiety disorder.

It is important to understand that managing anxiety in any intensity is quite possible, it is also important to understand that even though the symptoms might make you uncomfortable, the symptoms are actually not dangerous. It is in fact almost always treatable through therapy and exercises, i.e. you yourself can rid yourself of anxiety.

Here are some answers to some questions you might have about this book:

1. **What is this book about?** This book is about anxiety and panic disorders and how to get rid of them.

2. **Should I buy this book only if I have anxiety and panic attacks?** No. Anxiety is an emotion. It is felt by all people in the world, you should read this book as a counter-measure to both normal anxiety and anxiety disorders.

3. **Is there actually a way to cure anxiety?** Well as it turns out, a combination of therapy and exercises have succeeded in treating anxiety to degrees more than medication. Most doctors say so. So, instead of spending money on medication, spend money in improving your mental and physical control over anxiety and panic attacks i.e. buy this book. But the author (me) is not a doctor and is merely writing for educational purposes.

4. **Do you have other FREE resources that I can use?** Sure, visit cognitt.com to get tons of articles on many problems and solutions including anxiety and panic attacks.

This book is here to provide you information about anxiety and panic attacks as well as strategies and techniques to deal with them. The book consists of four chapters based on various aspects of dealing with the said problem. The first two chapters deal with knowing anxiety and how to diagnose yourself, whereas chapter 3 and 4 deal with actually getting down to ridding yourself of them. There is also a resources page which has bonus content at the end of the book.

Anxiety can take a toll on one's life. The life of a person with an anxiety disorder is not a life which can be called fun. It can result in ruined relationships and takes out the joy of being alone or enjoying the company of others.

Sometimes the attacks come when you least expect them to. Sometimes it looks like everything is okay but the attack is actually going on internally. It might feel like something significant is required, a catalyst, to get rid of your anxiety. That catalyst might be you, your initiative. Anxiety and panic attacks can be a whole lot easier to deal with if you have a plan. Look at long term relief that you will achieve by going through short term pain and you will rid yourself of your suffering.

On the other side, we look at panic attacks and how obnoxious they can be, people describe the feeling of having a panic attack as dying. It is important to realize when you are going to have a panic attack.

CHAPTER 1
WHAT IS ANXIETY?

Anxiety is an emotion in many but a disorder in a few. This chapter is dedicated to the triggers of anxiety and its types.

There are multiple ways and triggers for feeling anxious:

Anxiety of not getting what you want: Not getting something that is meaningful to you and constant denial from it can cause anxiety.

Anxiety of losing something: Something that is close to you or something that you cherish. You feel like that something is in jeopardy or will be in jeopardy if you do/don't do something.

Anxiety of something in the future: Future events that stress you like public speeches, performance related things or things that you dread will happen and potentially affect your life adversely.

What is the thing that you want most in life? Most of us never ask ourselves that questions. Fear of never having that thing, or uncertainty about it can cause anxiety as well as depression.

Anxiety can come from anything and it is important to solve the trigger. It can also stem from traumatic experiences, and negative reinforcements i.e. feeding negative thoughts and failure again and again till the person doubts himself or starts feeling anxious about the prospect of doing something. One of the biggest example of negative reinforcements which cause anxiety is negative parenting.

In the case of negative parenting, if the parents scold the child for making a mistake, then the child will logically think that making mistakes is bad, which could not only stunt the growth and learning of the child, but the child might show excessive avoidance of making mistakes, this can easily turn into anxiety where the child is constantly in fear of making a wrong move, and will not only become paralyzed in decision making but could also develop an anxiety disorder. It is easy to see how anxiety can thus subtract from one's life, experiences, possibilities and abilities. It is also easy to see that negative experiences can fuel anxiety.

Anxiety is characterized with excessive worry or fear, which hampers in the way of a normal life. When you constantly think negative thoughts, your brain function decreases. This in turn produces a debilitating effect on the way of life in a person who has anxiety. Stress from overthinking also contributes to chances of anxiety. All these factors have respective symptoms or contribute to symptoms which is discussed later in the book.

Five Anxiety disorders

As we learn about anxiety, it is important to know at least the most common forms of anxiety disorders. Given below are the five most common types of anxiety faced by people:

Obsessive-compulsive disorder (OCD): Obsessions can encompass the things that bother a person. The compulsion is the need to act on these botherations. It is very intrusive and destructive to the person's life. Psychotherapy and medications are treatments for this disorder.

Generalized anxiety disorder (GAD): GAD causes the person to internalize the suffering through anxiety. The treatment is similar to treatment to OCD. Cognitive behavior therapy and relaxation techniques, as well as mindfulness are used to treat this disorder.

Social anxiety disorder: Related to social interactions. Can be like fear of public speaking, approaching to talk to people. The sufferer can face severe self-consciousness. Therapy and medication are treatments for this disorder.

Panic disorder: Rests solely on panic attacks, heart palpitation, racing pulse, intense fear. There is usually no rhyme and reason to the timing of the attacks. Medications with therapy are treatments for this disorder.

Post-traumatic stress disorder (PTSD): It is the result of a traumatic event or even a series of traumatic events. The person might get panic attacks as well as phobias related to the traumatic event/events. They can lash out in certain situations. Medication and therapy are treatments for this disorder.

As you can see all these types of anxiety disorders respond to therapy. This shows that you yourself can change your struggle.

I would advise getting a doctor to diagnose whichever type of anxiety you have. If you already know which type of disorder you have will have you at an advantage, even though the steps given in this book are meant to be effective for all forms of anxiety.

GAD: Generalized anxiety disorder

GAD is one of the most common disorder form of anxiety. It is for this reason that we look briefly at this anxiety disorder. There are many misconceptions regarding this disorder and it is important to acknowledge and clear these misconceptions.

Before GAD was discovered, for many years people complained of symptoms very similar to depression but it wasn't depression that they were facing - it was Generalized Anxiety Disorder (GAD). People suffer from the constant sense that something terrible is going to happen. They visualize all the things that can go wrong in any situation.

Assumptions about GAD

There are some assumptions that should be acknowledged and cleared.

People feel that GAD is out of their control: In other words, they feel that GAD is something that they cannot control, which is simply not true. I will show you how to tackle this and disprove the assumption in the following chapters.

People with severe GAD might never be able have normal lives: On the contrary, people with severe GAD actually might be able to live fairly normal lives if they make changes suited to their condition such as medication and therapy.

The sensations will never change: It might worsen or improve over time, depending on how you deal with it. The more you live in fear and run away from it, the worse it will get, the moment you face your anxiety is the moment it will start to get better.

CHAPTER 2
HOW TO KNOW IF YOU HAVE ANXIETY

T he most common method to know if you have anxiety is to compare your symptoms with the typical symptoms of anxiety. There are two types of symptoms/signs when you have anxiety. They are physical symptoms and behavioral symptoms. Any combination of the given signs could be evidence of an anxiety disorder.

Symptoms for anxiety

In order to get rid of anxiety we must first know the symptoms that are normally experienced with anxiety. Given below are some of the most common symptoms.

Physical Symptoms

1. Restlessness
2. Sleeplessness
3. Hyperventilation
4. Heart palpitation

5. Clenched jaw or teeth grinding
6. Shaking of hands
7. Sweating

The above are the physical symptoms that you might show when you are feeling anxiety, but there are some behavioral anxiety symptoms as well.

Behavioral Symptoms

You disappear without a notice: The want of personal space forces you to remove yourself from social settings with the least amount of fuss, by simply vanishing.

You freak out over the time it takes for someone to respond to your text: You start overthinking about what you messaged someone and if it was too weird, rude or annoying. You relate time taken to respond, to the notion that you have done something wrong.

You over-check things: Over-checking can be a dead giveaway of anxiety. Even though you know exactly where you have kept something, you tend to check and check again, because you feel like that item is not there or that you have misplaced it or forgotten where it was kept.

You don't go to parties: Even though you might like the prospect of having fun, you doubt yourself about making friends and succeeding in conversations and therefore avoid parties altogether.

Certain dates give you anxiety: Remembering traumatic moments and events in your life and feeling depressed can be a sign of anxiety.

You hold on to your phone too much: Holding on to your phone can be a sign of avoiding social contact. Even fidgeting with your phone for no reason can be a sign of anxiety.

You don't make new friends: You overthink what to say, what impression to make, and sometimes even avoid chatting with people as you think that you can't possibly leave a good impression.

You dread school work/office work: Even though you have done it thousands of times, the pressure of meeting a deadline might be activating anxiety.

You are clinging in a relationship: You think about the person too much and too many times. Thinking about what you have done wrong, and what could have done better. While this is not that big of a sign, it could still mean that you could have anxiety.

You fail in making plans: You overthink the situation, the place the setting and try to make it perfect. So you fail in making any plans at all.

You rehearse what you're going to say before talking on the phone: This is similar to rehearsing conversations, but the lack of visual feedback from the person's face might heighten your anxiety.

You need to be alone: You don't feel like being around people and feel like you need space.

Sidenote: If you are liking this book, can you **leave a review** for it on Amazon? It will really help my book.

CHAPTER 3
OVERCOMING ANXIETY

Active changes in your life have to be made in order to manage anxiety. It is possible to deal with and lessen the symptoms, by accepting that it is a part of you and knowing that you can deal with it through taking these measures.

Those who are adept in mindfulness and cognitive behavior therapy have a greater control over activity in the part of their brain responsible for concentration and mind-wandering, so it is important to practice those types of therapy. Apart from therapy, given below is a table with questions relating to your anxiety and some steps, called action steps, that you can take.

Question	Response
1. What symptoms do you feel?	
2. Do you feel confident in diagnosing when you are in a panic attack quickly?	
3. Do you think that panic attacks are dangerous?	
4. Do you trust your mind and body to cope through a panic attack?	
5. How many times do you get a panic attack/ per month	

Directions

First fill in all the responses in the table. Then follow the action steps given below. These steps are measures that can help you manage your anxiety. If you want a printable version of the table above then go to the Resources page.

Action Steps

Know that fear is normal: Fear is natural. It is hardwired into you to protect yourself. You need to learn to overcome that fear, you need to feel it but have the power to overpower it. Fear is an emotion. You have 100% control over your emotions and how they affect your mind.

Face the fear head on: It is an effective countermeasure against fear and anxiety. Imagine just facing your fears gallantly. It will send a subliminal message to your brain that there is no actual danger, as you have already embraced the fear and proved that it is nothing.

Be proactive: What do you focus on when you feel fear? It can determine how you feel about the task. What kind of language patterns do you use? What do you say to yourself? Are your thought empowering or limiting? Break these patterns and proactively try and put yourself into a positive mental pattern.

Abundance of tools to deal with anxiety: There are many methods and tools to deal with anxiety, including this book. You can use mindfulness, cognitive behavior therapy, meditation and consultation from a doctor to battle anxiety.

Believe: Self-belief and self-love are two of the most powerful ingredients to overcoming anxiety of all kinds. We worry because we think that we are not capable of dealing with the 'bad' that might happen to us. If you trust yourself to deal with any outcome whatsoever, then you have succeeded in eliminating a big chunk of your fear.

Don't think too much about the future: It is important for you to accept the fact that you will face anxiety attacks in the future. It is of no benefit to worry about them. Thinking about the next attack will probably worsen it.

Don't overthink situations: Overthinking situations can cause anxiety as you run through multiple scenarios and worry about the outcome.

Don't snap: Pushing yourself to getting something can be a cause of anxiety. The prospect of not getting it can eat away at your mental strength.

Meditate: Meditate for 20 minutes a day. Focus on your breathing while meditating.

Take action: If something is worrying you do something about it, don't let it decide your fate. Jump into action without thinking too much. People who feel like they have control over their lives have better mental health.

Understand your symptoms: Describe the physical sensation related to your nervous emotion and fear. This will help identify the most common signs of when you are going through an anxiety attack.

Focus on long term benefits: It might take some time for you to reap benefits of the given methods, but it will be worth it when you can manage your anxiety well.

Face your anxiety and embrace it: Embrace the feeling of anxiety, because running away will only worsen the situation.

Know that your life depends only on you: If you overestimate how others really affect your life, you give away your choice and how you respond to someone. Stop overthinking your interactions with someone, they are not so important as to cause you anxiety.

Don't have self-pity: Unhealthy beliefs and self-pity can keep you from finding a solution, as you will just be fixated on the problem. It is upon you and only you to take care yourself and take charge of your life. Do you want to lessen your anxiety? Well then you should get on with it shouldn't you? Why do you want to keep suffering?

Anxiety is very common: Don't think that you are alone in your suffering. One in 14 people have anxiety, worldwide. Clearly you are not abnormal (god forbid if you think that). A LOT of people face anxiety in their daily lives.

Don't let other people decide your perception: The inherent issue is that we are dependent on the opinions of others. That is the cause of social anxiety. We need to understand what other people's opinions really mean and stop them from affecting us. People often project their own insecurities on others. What impacts us is if we start to believe the negative things that are said.

Chapter 4
How to Stop a Panic Attack

Have you ever experienced a panic attack? If you have then you probably want to stop it and end your struggle with them. This chapter is all about that.

If you look at your own experience, what happens when you try to stop a panic attack? It usually gets worse if you try to stop it. Why is that? In order to understand how to stop a panic attack, you need to know the symptoms and have a plan to counter to your panic attack, which is why I have made a symptom table along with action steps.

Symptoms

To start off you must identify the symptoms of your panic attack. Being mindful of symptoms will let you accurately diagnose when you have a panic attack and can then immediately take action.

Following are symptoms that a person going through a panic attack might face:

1. Palpitations
2. Sweating
3. Shaking or trembling
4. Feeling shortness of breath or smothering
5. Sensation of choking
6. Chest pains or tightness
7. Nausea or gastrointestinal problems
8. Dizziness, light-headedness, or feeling faint
9. Feeling hot or cold
10. Numbness or tingling sensations (paraesthesia)
11. Feeling detached from oneself or reality, known as de-personalization and de-realisation
12. Fear of "going crazy" or losing control
13. Fear of dying

Note the symptoms that you experience and add them to the list given below.

Question	Response
1. What symptoms do you feel?	
2. Do you feel confident in diagnosing when you are in a panic attack quickly?	
3. Do you think that panic attacks are dangerous?	
4. Do you trust your mind and body to cope through a panic attack?	
5. How many times do you get a panic attack/ per month	

Directions

First fill in all the responses in the table. Then follow the action steps given below. These steps are measures that can help you manage your panic attacks. If you want a printable version of the table above then go to the Resources page.

Action Steps

Identify symptoms: Answer question 1 with all the symptoms that you feel. Hyperventilation, palpitations and dry mouth correspond closely to symptoms of a panic attack. Identify and confirm that you are having a panic attack, follow the steps below.

Don't fuel your panic: The general mindset around panic attacks is negative. If you ticked question 3 i.e. you think that panic attacks are dangerous, then you need to change your mindset. When we think that panic attacks are bad, the feeling of panic is fueled. It is important to not have any thoughts regarding panic attacks in your head.

Do different things: A panic attack is just a physical sensation. Try your best to know that going through this suffering 24/7 is not compulsory, you can do different things, be productive and have fun as well. If you acknowledge that something is not inherently bad or good and that it is merely a sensation, then your panic will actually decrease. The sensation might persist but you will be at peace.

Don't associate panic attacks to negative thoughts: Often we get negative thoughts after getting panic attacks. We might think that there is something wrong with us for experiencing panic attacks and so on. Everyone in this world can feel the emotion that is anxiety, it is only the severity that might trouble people extensively.

Face your panic attacks head on: The key is when the individual no longer fears the prospect of a panic attack and is prepared to deal with it. Trust in yourself to deal with it. Panic attacks are inevitable, but you can quickly diagnose yourself and mitigate much of the suffering.

Know that worrying about it will change nothing: Instead of reacting negatively, move your attention to things you enjoy. It's not like constantly thinking about panic attacks will be of any help to you, you remain with the same level of anxiety and add the mental stress of thinking about it as well. Gradually, you will stop reacting negatively and start embracing your panic attacks.

Do not resist the panic attack: Trying to do so will only worsen the panic attack. It is extremely difficult to not think about something when you know that you shouldn't think about it. Know this fact and spare yourself the struggle in the midst of a panic attack.

Trust yours body and mind: This relates to question 4. Don't worry about your body being unable to handle a panic attack. Your body is naturally capable of this fight and flight reactions through evolution. Trust in yourself and your body's capability to bear through the symptoms. There is a resilience in us which can tide us over any situation, including panic attacks.

Do not fear future panic attacks: Be open to having future panic attacks, because they are going to happen anyway, trust yourself in handling these future panic attacks.

Don't be embarrassed about your attacks: Embarrassment felt through panic attacks will heighten the symptoms. Don't feel embarrassed about this. Would you feel sad and embarrassed if you had a severe cold and you were suffering because of it? You wouldn't because there is nothing shameful in that, know that it is the same for panic attacks.

Breathe and count: Not only will you not do something stupid in haste. You will also shift your thoughts from your attack towards breathing consciously. You will also gain time to realize that you are in a panic attack and that you need to follow your plan that you made earlier.

Find the root cause: Find what is affecting you and triggering your anxiety. Avoid or eradicate the trigger any time you come across it.

Grow in knowledge: Instead of just running away, deal with it and learn about it as much as you can. Knowledge in this scenario can be one your greatest weapons against panic attacks.

Short term pain vs long term gain: Focus on the long term results and ending your suffering for good. Sure, it will be uncomfortable at first, but it will never be dangerous or even too hard. Trade in your discomfort for the long term ending of your suffering.

CONCLUSION

I hope this book was able to guide you on how to manage your anxiety and panic attacks. The next step is to apply the methods given in this book and see results in the long run.

Finally, if you enjoyed this book, then I'd like to ask you for a favor, would you be kind enough to **leave a review** for this book on Amazon? It'd be greatly appreciated! Reviews can really help promote the book and every review is valuable. Also be sure to take advantage of the extra material in the Resources page.

Bonus: Be sure to check out the preview of, *'Clutter: Living Life And Leaving The Rest'* by Stotra Anubhav in the next page.

Thank you and good luck!

CLUTTER

Living Life And Leaving The Rest

CHAPTER-1
HOW TO APPROACH
CLUTTER

One of the biggest problems while decluttering and getting rid of items is to deal with people's emotions. People often attach some memory or emotion to things that they have owned for a certain period of time so it is difficult for them to personally get rid of them. Their friends find it easy because they have no attachment. So it is a good idea to get a friend or a professional to come to your home and assess the situation objectively.

Along with bringing some company, add a bit of objectivity to yourself as well. Use a rule or an algorithm to which you can adhere. Then you will have a clear idea of which items you need to discard and which ones need to stay. Our own algorithm is given at the end of the chapter.

Getting rid of clutter takes time. Anyone offering an instant solution to this problem is probably taking you for a ride. Doing it over a week or even a weekend is possible, but it will be stressful, mentally and physically exhausting, and might not be up to our expectations. Create a routine for decluttering by giving an hour of your time every week to decluttering. Be honest to this schedule and consistently put in the one hour, and you will see change.

Some people feel like that they do not have enough time in their lives to deal with clutter. Rearrange your schedule to make time for decluttering. Wake up an hour early if you have to. Decluttering is a skill that you can learn and apply throughout your life, so you simply have to stick with it. If it is affecting your life then it surely deserves your time.

Removing clutter can seem like an absolute chore. But it might not be a chore if you succeed in setting up a routine.

There is a difference between clutter and organization.

Organizing is when you arrange your possessions in a systematic manner. Decluttering is simply getting rid of stuff that does not have any value in your life.

Having clutter does not mean that you are messy and being messy doesn't mean that you have clutter. Organizing is temporary and decluttering is rather permanent, since the stuff that you got rid of is gone forever. But even decluttering is temporary when looked at over a long period of time. This is because the things that you own and acquire will eventually become clutter, as your personal likings and priorities will change.

There is a difference between decluttering and minimalism.

Minimalism in a broad way can be described as living with the bare essentials - having as less possessions as possible. If it is not necessary for your life then it cannot be included in a minimalist lifestyle. Many people have a different meaning attached to minimalism but it always has the theme of having only the bare essentials.

Decluttering is actually considered the first step towards minimalism. While decluttering we move away from stuff that we have but don't derive any value from, towards things that are of value to us. Decluttering concerns things that have value in our lives, minimalism is about need. Clearly decluttering is not minimalism.

Liked this chapter? Go to
https://amzn.to/2E1Uxp5 to buy this book!

Resources

To get the printable version of the table in chapters 3 and 4 go to:

https://cognitt.com/anxiety

www.ingramcontent.com/pod-product-compliance
Lightning Source LLC
Chambersburg PA
CBHW060531280326
41933CB00014B/3128